• LEARNING HOW •
BMX Biking

BY
SUE BOULAIS

Bancroft-Sage Publishing

601 Elkcam Circle, Suite C-7, P.O. 355 Marco, Florida 33969-0355 USA

• L E A R N I N G   H O W •
BMX Biking

AUTHOR
SUE BOULAIS

EDITED BY
JODY JAMES

DESIGNED BY
CONCEPT and DESIGN

PHOTO CREDITS

Action Photos: Pages 9a, 26.
All Sport: Page 44
Michael King - Page 28;
Patrick Massias - Page 35;
Mike Powell - Page 11;
Pascal Rondeau - Pages 5, 7, 9b, 48c;
Budd Symes - Page 31.
Gallery Nineteen: Brent Johnson - Pages 15, 25, 29a, 31a, 33, 37, 40, 48b.
Jim Kirk: Pages 27, 29b, 48a.
Brad McDonald: Pages 39, 41, 43.
Unicorn Stock Photos: Les Van - Cover, Pages 13, 45.
Diagrams By: Concept and Design - Pages 10, 17, 18, 19, 20, 21, 23.

ACKNOWLEDGMENTS

Special thanks to Pat Menton and Craig Skorr for their help and assistance regarding BMX biking.

TABLE OF CONTENTS

**LIBRARY OF CONGRESS
CATALOGING-IN-PUBLICATION DATA**

Boulais, Sue.
  Learning how: BMX biking / by Sue Boulais; edited by Jody James; illustrated by
Concept and Design.
      p.   cm. – (Learning how sports)
  Summary: Describes various aspects of bicycle motocross including the history of the
sport, the equipment, tracks, rules, safety, and riding techniques.
  ISBN 0-944280-36-6 (lib. bdg.) – ISBN 0-944280-41-2 (pbk.)
    1. Bicycle motocross – Juvenile literature. [1. Bicycle motocross.]   I. James, Jody.
II. Title. III. Series.
  GV1049.3.B68   1991
  796.6'2–dc20   91-27219
                                                                                    CIP
                                                                                    AC

**International Standard
Book Number:**
Library Binding 0-944280-36-6
Paperback Binding 0-944280-41-2

**Library of Congress
Catalog Card Number:**
91-27219

CHAPTER ONE:

Introduction

In 1969, a new kind of bicycle soared across America's movie screens. It looked a lot like a motorcycle. It was small and tough and low to the ground. It had knobby tires and high, motorcycle-like handlebars. Best of all, the new bike didn't just speed over the ground. It seemed to fly through the air!

The bicycles—and their riders—appeared in a movie about motorcycles. On their special bikes, the kids did all the fancy, exciting moves and tricks done by trained professional motorcycle riders. They raced their bicycles around a dirt racetrack. They jumped over tree stumps. They slid around corners. They skidded to a sideways stop, sending up dust sprays. They popped wheelies. Motorcycle moves on bicycles! Wow!

The new bikes and the kids weren't in the movie for very long. But it was long enough. A new sport was born: Bicycle Motocross, or BMX.

The tough little bikes, made by Schwinn Bicycle Company, were called Stingrays™. Schwinn had made the bikes especially for the movie. The company had designed the bikes extra-tough. The little machines had to "hang together" when their riders performed those motorcycle tricks.

The BMX bike created an exciting new world of fun and competition.

The Stingrays were just what young bike riders had been looking for. Boys and girls all across America had been trying to imitate the moves and tricks of motorcycle riders for several years. But they had tried the moves and tricks on regular two-wheeled bikes. And regular bikes couldn't take it.

Pop wheelies? Jump street curbs? Skid and slide on a bike's side? Kids had found their bikes sliding out of control. Bicycle frames broke in half. Wheels and fenders bent. Spokes and pedals cracked.

But the new bikes didn't break or bend or crack. Before long, they could be seen in almost every neighborhood in America. Kids were popping wheelies, flying over curbs and hedges, and sliding to a stop inches from those watching.

For a while, BMX riding was just unorganized neighborhood fun. But some riders became careless about where they rode. They became careless of other people's property, of other people's safety. Some riders weren't even very careful about their own safety.

Parents and other concerned adults began to organize special places for riders to practice their moves. Special BMX racetracks began to appear, first in the Southeast and Southwest, then in other areas of the United States. Bicycle riding and racing clubs such as the National Bicycle League and the American Bicycle Association also began to set up special BMX activities for young riders.

By the late 1970s, BMX riding and racing were widespread and popular with young American bicyclists. Bicycle and racing standards had been established. Safety equipment had been introduced and was required for every racer.

Some BMX riders had even found new and daring tricks to do on their tough little bikes. These young athletes introduced *freestyle* BMX: acrobatics and gymnastics on wheels.

In the 1980s, BMX spread to Canada, England, and Europe. It wheeled into the Orient, Africa, and Australia. Wherever boys and girls rode bicycles, BMX showed up. A special organization, the International Bicycle Motocross Federation (IBMXF), was set up in the Netherlands.

Today, many young American bicyclists take part in BMX races and freestyle competitions. But many, many more ride and "fly" their bikes just for fun. Jumping a puddle is a good way to stay dry on the way to school. Popping wheelies is great while running errands. And any open space just calls out a challenge for some dodging and sliding.

BMX races and freestyle competitions are held world-wide.

CHAPTER TWO:

BMX Racing

Bicycle motocross is a lot like motorcycle motocross. It's a fast race on a rough, tight dirt track. Instead of an engine driven by horsepower though, you're racing on a bicycle driven by leg power.

BMX racing combines skill and **tactics**. A rider must handle a bike well, making all the right moves easily and quickly. But a rider also has to be able to plan a strategy for winning a race, then change those plans quickly if necessary.

Motos (races) begin at the top of a hill or ramp. Riders line up behind the starting board, or gate. The front wheels of their bikes touch the board. As soon as the board drops, the riders shoot down their racing lanes. Each biker aims for the **holeshot**, the leading position on the first turn. At the bottom of the start hill, the track narrows, and passing a competitor isn't easy.

Even though a BMX racetrack is short, it has plenty of jumps, bumps, and turns. Riders face **sweepers**, turns so sharp and flat that riders must slow down and put one foot almost to the ground for balance. They pedal up and across **tabletops**, flat, elevated areas that end in bone-bruising jumps. They fly around **berms**, curving walls of dirt around inside banked corners. They leap across **whoop-de-doos**, three jumps one right after another. Now and again stretches of level track let riders build up speed.

As the starting board or gate, drops the riders shoot down their racing lanes.

Each biker aims for the holeshot, or lead position on the first turn.

Sweepers, berms, and whoop-de-doos are just some of the **obstacles** that a BMX racer meets on a racetrack. Although most racetracks are 700 to 900 feet long, a typical race may not take even a full minute. But the last straightaway to the finish line can seem miles long to racers!

BMX motos have events for riders ages 6 to over 16. Riders are grouped by age, then by skill and experience. Sets of eight riders in each age group compete in three motos. Riders have different starting positions in each moto.

A Typical Track Layout

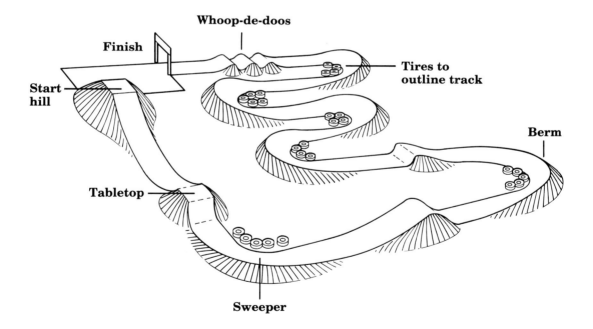

A BMX track will have many obstacles like sweepers, berms and whoop-de-doos.

Racers get the same number of points as their finishing position: one point for first place, two points for second, etc. At the end of three motos, the four riders with the fewest points qualify for the next round. Final winners often are awarded trophies or other prizes. But many races are run just for the competition.

Some rules for official BMX meets vary from race to race. But some rules are always the same. Racers must always register and pay an entry fee. All entered bikes must be inspected to be sure that they are safe and correctly adjusted.

During the race, riders cannot leave the track or cut corners to get ahead. They cannot push or kick an opponent or use bad language. Racers are not permitted to act in an unsportsmanlike manner after a moto, either. Displays of bad temper or behavior can disqualify a biker any time before, during, or after a moto.

These riders are racing over whoop-de-doos heading for the finish line.

CHAPTER THREE:

BMX Freestyle

BMX freestylers "go for the ozone." Some call it **taking air**, or *getting airborne*. Whatever they call it, every freestyler tries to take bike and self high into the air. Freestylers begin with ground moves, but their aim is "up there."

To get airborne, freestylers need speed and height. They use **ramps** of different sizes, as well as concrete **quarterpipes** and skateboarding bowls. Flying up the ramps, or down the quarterpipes, freestylers pick up the speed they need. At the end of the ramps, they just keep flying—into unbelievable spirals and turns and leaps.

But freestylers do incredible tricks on the ground, too. **Frame stands**, body balances, standing and sitting leaps, one-hand **wheelstands** and kickturns, no-hand **bar hops**, no-feet endos, bouncing pogos: there's almost no limit to the stunts and tricks of daredevil freestylers.

Freestyle competitions are organized by age group. Riders show off their stuff first on the ground by doing a set of *compulsory exercises*. Every rider must do these moves. Then comes the voluntary or freestyle routine. In this part of the competition, "the sky's the limit."

Freestyling isn't for every BMX bike owner. It takes days, sometimes weeks, to get a trick just right. It can also take plenty of bruises and a broken bone or two. But serious freestylers love it—broken bones and all!

BMX freestylers "take air". To get airborne, freestylers need speed and height. They use ramps of different sizes as well as skateboarding bowls.

CHAPTER FOUR:

The BMX Riding and Racing Bicycle

What makes a BMX bicycle different from a standard bicycle? A BMX bike has the same *line* as a motorcycle. Its triangle-shaped *frame* sits low to the ground and is slanted sharply to the rear, like that of a motorcycle. A BMX bike has high, braced handlebars. The handlebars, too, slant more to the back, like a motorcycle's.

BMX bikes are *stripped down*. They don't have any parts just for decoration. They have no fenders and only a single gear. Parts that aren't necessary mean more weight—and BMX bikes are built as light as possible.

The metal parts of BMX bikes are made of **alloys** to keep them as light as possible. Very strong steel is mixed with lighter metals such as aluminum and chrome. The alloy that comes from the mixture has the strength of steel and the lightness of aluminum and chrome.

BMX tires are also like a motorcycle's. They have a **knobby** tread that grips the dirt. With these tires, riders can take tight corners, slide, and stop without losing control of the bike.

A BMX bike has the same line as this motorcycle.

The BMX triangle-shaped frame sits low to the ground and is slanted sharply to the rear like that of a motorcycle.

Learning About a BMX Bike

Smaller, tougher, lighter: that's how a BMX bike is different overall from a standard bicycle. Let's take a closer look at a BMX bike and its parts. Knowing what these parts are and what they do is important when you are looking for a bike to buy.

Frame

The frame is the bike's *foundation*. All other bike parts are fastened in some way to the frame. If the frame isn't strong, the bike won't hold up when you ride or race.

A BMX frame is shaped like a triangle. Tubes make the top and one side of the triangle. The other side of the triangle is made by the *seat mast*, the tube that holds the seat. The tubes should be smoothly welded together with no bumps anywhere on the frame.

Sometimes the frame may have extra metal braces called *gussets* at the corners where the tubes meet. The gussets make the frame stronger.

Check the bike's tag or frame to find out what materials the frame is made of. All parts of the frame should be made of a steel or aluminum alloy. The frame of a good bike is usually made of *chrome-moly* steel (an alloy of steel made with metals called *chromium* and *molybdenum*).

Handlebars

The high-rising handlebars steer the bike. A brace bar is usually placed at about the middle of the handlebars to make them stronger. Handlebars also have rubber *handgrips*.

Handlebars can be between two feet (24 inches) and 28 inches wide. Choose a width that's comfortable for you.

Gooseneck

The gooseneck is sometimes called the *stem*. It's the superstrong piece that holds the handlebars. The gooseneck also holds the *forks*. (Forks hold the bike's front wheel in place.) A BMX gooseneck always has at least two—but most often four—bolts that grip the handlebars. The bolts keep the handlebars from twisting or slipping.

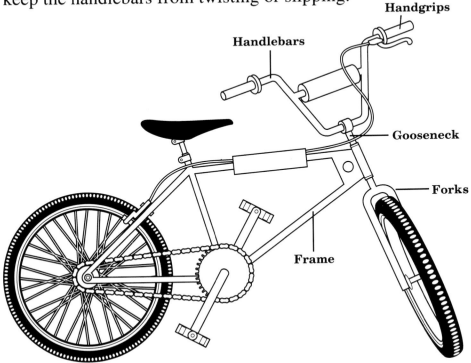

Handgrips

Handlebars

Gooseneck

Forks

Frame

Wheels and Tires

BMX wheels are usually about 20" in diameter and have 28 spokes. Some wheels may have 32 or 36 spokes. The extra ones are made from very strong steel and give the wheels more support.

BMX bicycle tires are very much like the tires on a lightweight dirt-riding motorcycle. The knobby *tread* bites into the loose dirt, sand, or gravel that tops most BMX trails and raceways. On many tires, the *sidewalls* also have knobby tread. Having tread on the sidewalls gives you a good grip on the dirt or sand surface when you lay your bike over on a turn.

This drawing illustrates the tread and spoked wheel for a BMX racing bike. Having tread on the sidewalls gives you a good grip on dirt or sand.

Drivetrain

These are the parts that make your bike go: pedals, cranks, chainwheels, and chain. Pedals transfer your foot power into bike power. BMX bike pedals are always a *rattrap* style. Rattrap pedals have ridged bars that fit your feet. The ridges have teeth called *studs* that keep your feet from slipping off.

The pedals shouldn't be any wider than you need for comfort and a good fit. If the bike's pedals are too long, they'll dig into the ground when you lean your bike in for turns.

BMX pedals have no toe clips, as some standard bikes do. When you're riding BMX-style, you'll need to move your feet back and forth from the pedals to the ground very quickly. Toe holds, of course, stop you from moving your feet quickly.

Cranks are the pieces that attach the pedals. The longer the cranks are, the more power you can produce when you pedal. The more power you produce, the faster you can go. However, if the cranks are too long, your leg muscles will have to work harder to get them turning. For the best results, find a bike with medium-length cranks.

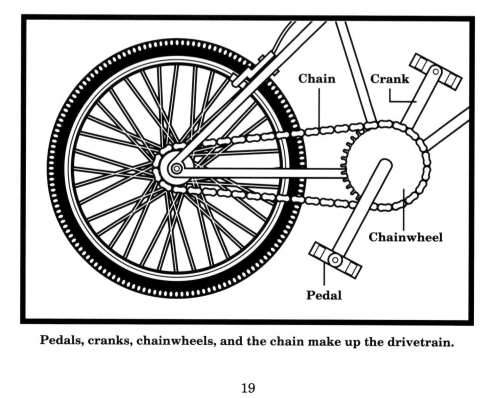

Pedals, cranks, chainwheels, and the chain make up the drivetrain.

Chainwheels are the larger and smaller metal wheels with teeth that hold the chain. Chainwheels are also called *sprockets*. The chainwheels control the bike's *gear ratio*—which determines how fast and how hard you must pedal to achieve a certain speed.

Sometimes chainwheels are built into the bicycle, but just as often they are removable. Built-in chainwheels are set in the proper gear ratio at the factory.

The *chain* is the continuous loop of metal that ties the drivetrain together. It fits over the teeth on the chainwheels. Some chains are closed at the factory and exactly fit the bikes they're on. Other chains have *master links*. These chains can be taken apart and made longer or shorter by adding or taking out links.

All parts of the drive chain should be light, but strongly-made. The chain should be shiny and should feel solid.

Brakes

Most BMX bikes have **caliper brakes** (hand brakes) placed near the handlebar grips. Caliper brakes slow or stop the bike by squeezing the tire rims. All BMX bikes have rear brakes. Some have front brakes, too, but these aren't necessary.

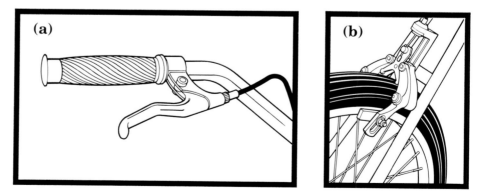

The (a) caliper brakes (or hand brakes) slow or stop the bike by squeezing the (b) tire rim.

Seat

The seat on a BMX bike is often called the *saddle*. The saddle is hard and narrow, and sits on top of the seat post. Seat post and saddle are firmly held together by a special clamp. The clamp loosens so that you can move the seat post up and down to get the saddle to a comfortable height.

Protective Pads

These pads help protect you from being hurt. Pads fit over the top tube of the bike's frame, the handlebar cross brace, and the handlebar stem.

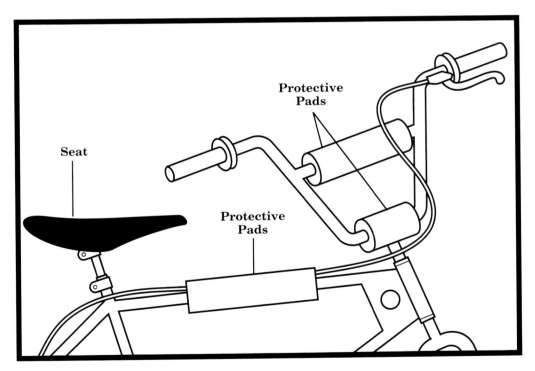

Protective pads on the bike's frame, handlebar cross brace, and handlebar stem are used to help prevent injuries.

The BMX Freestyle Bike

As tough and sturdy as a BMX racing bike is, a BMX freestyle bike is tougher. It has to be, to take the pounding that goes with the high jumps, heavy landings, and other moves of BMX freestyle.

For the most part, a BMX freestyle bike has the same parts as a racing bike. However, the freestyler is different in the following ways:

Brakes

A freestyle bike has *three* sets of brakes: front and rear calipers and a **coaster brake**. Front calipers are necessary for certain tricks, particularly front **endos**. Rear calipers are necessary while doing any ramp maneuvers. The coaster brake in neutral position lets the bike go forward or backward without the wheels turning.

Wheels

The best freestyling wheels are a blend of a special plastic and nylon. They are very strong and can take the rough landings that are a part of freestyle riding. They are also easy to take care of and keep clean.

Tires

Freestyling is usually done on hard *asphalt* or concrete surfaces. So it needs a very different kind of tire from the BMX racing bike used on dirt tracks. Freestyling tires need more pressure and less tread. Some freestylers use regular street tires; others use tires with a *snake belly* tread. Some use stadium-type tires. Racing knobbies slide out during important moves—not a thing a freestyler wants.

Freestyling wheels are very strong and the tires need more pressure and less tread than racing tires.

Pedals

Pedals take constant slamming in freestyling. So look for *steel* pedals, not alloys. Steel pedals can take almost any beating.

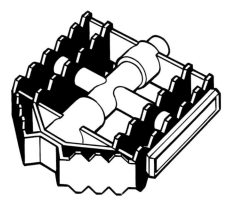

Steel pedals are very important for freestyle biking. They can take almost any beating.

Accessories

As you become a better and better freestyler, you'll want to try ramp and tunnel stunts. Many such tricks need special equipment, such as stands or pegs. You don't need any of these at the start, however. A good-quality bike will get you started.

Shopping for Your BMX Bike

Once you know the parts of a BMX bike and how they are put together, visit some bike shops and look around. Compare the different-priced bikes. Check all the parts to be sure they are strongly made and attached well. Look for smooth, continuous welding on the bike's frame.

Rotate the wheels to be sure they turn quietly, steadily, and smoothly. They shouldn't wobble, hesitate, or stick as they turn.

Work the brakes to see if they do their job quickly. Check also to be sure that the brake shoes clamp equally on both sides of the tire.

Look carefully at the bike's *finish*, or paint job. The paint should be smooth and carefully layered. Cracked paint around joints could mean a poor weld. Double-check around decals and stickers to be sure they aren't hiding a mistake.

When you've chosen the bike you think you want, talk to the dealer or shop owner. A good bike dealer should know about BMX bikes and should be able to tell you about adjustments your bike might need. He or she should also ask you questions about the kind of BMX riding you want to do. The dealer can take that information, along with your size, and be sure that the bike you've chosen is the right one for you.

Shop carefully when purchasing a BMX bike. A good bike dealer can help you choose the bike that is correct for you and the type of riding you want to do.

Caring for Your BMX Bike

Caring for your BMX bike is a two-part job: keep it clean and keep it tuned up. Regular cleaning and tune-ups will help your bike travel a long way for a long time!

Your bike should be tuned, oiled and cleaned often to last a long time.

Clean your bike as often as it needs it. Always clean it after you've ridden it in a race or in dirt or mud. Use soap and water, or window cleaner. (Never use gasoline. It ruins your bike's finish.) Make sure that you get all dirt and grit out of the drive chain and off the brake shoes.

Have your bike tuned and *lubricated* (oiled) before and after a race. The bicycle shop owner can do a tune-up for you or recommend someone who can.

Always clean and oil your bike after a race or when riding in dirt or mud.

Riding Your BMX Bicycle Safely

Riding a BMX bike is always fun and exciting. You may be on your way to school or to the store for your parents. You may be **thrashing** (goofing around) along your neighborhood block or headed flat out toward the final whoop-de-doos on a BMX racetrack. Wherever you are and whatever you're doing with your "flying" bike, you're having a good time.

Good BMX riders make their good times even better by dressing and riding as safely as possible. Always wear the following equipment when you ride your BMX bike.

Always wear the proper equipment when riding your BMX bike.

Helmet

The single most important piece of safety equipment is a BMX bicycle helmet. A BMX helmet is made of very strong but very lightweight fiberglass. Inside is a padded, nylon-covered liner that fits snugly over your head. A strong chin strap holds the helmet on through even the most daring jumps or crashes.

A helmet is required in both BMX racing and freestyle competitions. But most serious BMX riders always wear their helmets whenever they ride their bikes. You never know when you might want to leap over a tree stump or do a reverse skid!

Mouthguard

A mouthguard is a light, plastic "cage" that covers your mouth and guards your lips and teeth. Many helmets come with built-in mouthguards. Other helmets have fasteners to which you can attach a mouthguard.

The most important piece of safety equipment is a helmet.

A mouthguard is needed to cover and protect your lips and teeth.

Shirt

Even the best BMX riders **crash and burn** (take a spill). Wearing a long-sleeved shirt can help protect your arms from bruises, cuts, and scratches.

Pants

The legs of your pants should fit tight and close to your legs. Loose pant legs can get oil and grease on them. More seriously, they can cause accidents by getting caught in your bike's chain. Straight-legged jeans are good pants for thrashing around town.

Shoes and Socks

Any running or jogging shoes with soft rubber soles are good footwear. Rubber soles won't slide off the rattrap pedals. Most BMX riders wear laced tennis shoes. You should also wear heavy socks to help protect your legs and ankles from getting banged up.

Competition Wear

When you compete in BMX races or freestyle displays, you must wear close fitting pants and shirts that have protective padding. Pants generally have padded knees and hips. Shirts have padded elbows. Both pants and shirts have zippers to keep clothing away from moving parts of the bike.

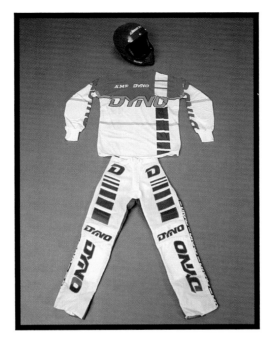

A good BMX shirt should have long sleeves to protect your arms from bruises and cuts. The pant legs should fit close to your legs to keep from getting caught in your bike's chain.

When competing in races or freestyle displays, close fitting pants and shirts with protective padding are a must.

CHAPTER FIVE

Doing Basic BMX Moves

You have your shiny new BMX bike. You have your new BMX bicycle helmet. You're dressed for action. You're ready to learn how to handle your new bike and do some fancy riding—**rad riding**, BMX riders call it.

To begin, ride your new bike around your yard or block. Be sure the seat height is comfortable and that your feet fit the pedals. Work the caliper brakes to get their "feel." Turn a couple of corners to see how your bike handles. Ride it for a while just to get used to your bike's lightness and easy handling.

While you're riding around your neighborhood, remember that you are a bicycle rider first and an acrobat on wheels second. Follow all safety rules. Ride on the right side of the road or street. Don't fight with cars or other cyclists about who has the right-of-way; yield to other vehicles. Watch for cars backing out of driveways. Be alert to traffic around you. Use your hand signals. Stick to bicycle lanes, if your neighborhood has them.

First, practice riding around a bend or corner. Keep the same distance from the curb all the time you're taking the turn. Once you can do that, ride around a tree or several trees. Again, try always to stay the same distance from the trees.

Keep your eyes open for places to practice some new moves. Long-time BMX riders call these moves thrashing or *hotdogging* or *styling*. You're learning how to handle your bike—and showing off a little at the same time.

When beginning, ride your new bike around your yard or block. You will want to get used to your bike's lightness and easy handling.

Control Moves: Stop, Corner, Skid, Slide

One important "control" move is stopping your bike so that the front wheel is "dead" on a line (stopped exactly on a line). Work this move up fairly slowly, or you'll stop so fast you *and* your bike will crash and burn. Each time you try this stop, pedal a little faster, and squeeze your calipers a little quicker. You may skid past your "stop" line the first few times. But you'll get the "feel" of the brakes in no time.

Now find a soft dirt or sand area and learn two more control moves: *cornering* and *skidding*. Cornering is going around a curve. Skidding is sliding on your tires while your tires aren't turning.

Knowing how to corner is really important in BMX racing. And the most important thing to learn in cornering is control. If you lose control, you skid, and skidding takes up time. Try to keep both feet on the pedals to keep up your speed. To keep your tires on the ground, try leaning *into* the corner. Keep practicing until you know how far you and your bike can lean before you start to skid.

If you feel like you're losing control, put your inside foot toward the ground—fast—to catch yourself. Try to keep pedaling with your outside foot.

Try some skids and **recoveries** "on purpose." Slant your bike over on its side and turn your handlebars until you feel the rear wheel start to slide out from under you. Recover (get out of the skid) by turning the handlebars *in the direction* of the skid and push down on the tires.

You might even want to try a *slide stop* (also called a panic stop). Pedal up to good speed. Lock your brakes and bring your bike to a controlled skidding stop. If you start to crash, let up on your brake to get your balance.

Ready to go for some of the basic "fancy" moves of both racers and freestylers? Four are shown in the rest of this book: wheelie, endo, bunny hop, and pogo jump. Practice each one until you can do it perfectly—no **wipeouts.** These moves are just the beginning.

So—PUT YOUR HELMET ON AND GO FOR IT!

If you feel you're losing control while cornering, put your inside foot toward the ground to catch yourself. Try to keep pedaling with your outside foot.

The Wheelie

Wheelies are one of the first moves every BMX rider learns. Doing a wheelie means you ride with the front wheel of your bike in the air. It's a move that shouldn't give you too much trouble. Your bike is light and was made for getting off the ground.

Do a wheelie at medium speed. Bend your arms a little and lean into your bike. Then move your body backwards on the saddle. At the same time, lift up on the handlebars. Practice until the shifting and pulling up happen smoothly and rhythmically.

Once you get your front wheel in the air, try to hold it by balancing on your back wheel. If you feel like you're going to fall over backwards, get one or both feet quickly on the ground. (Your front wheel will come down, too.) Bend your knees a little as you come down. This will help soften your landing. Then try again. When you can do a wheelie with no trouble, go on to the endo.

When doing a wheelie, you ride with the front wheel of your bike in the air.

The Endo

An endo is a wheelie in reverse. That means your rear wheel is off the ground. In freestyling, this move is called an *endo*. (In BMX racing, an *endo* is a "crash and burn" over the handlebars of your bike.)

To do an endo, you need something to stop your front wheel. Find something low, such as a curb. Ride toward it slowly, with both feet on the pedals. Just as your wheel hits against the stopper, raise your body off the seat. Push down and forward on the handlebars. The rear wheel of your bike will come up, and the front end will be stopped against the curb. You'll find yourself balanced over the front wheel. Hold yourself there for as long as you can.

Watch your speed on an endo. If you're going too fast when you reach the curb, you could be the one flying, not your bike. If you feel like you're losing control, get your feet back on the ground. Try it again at a slower speed.

When you've got the "feel" of a curb endo, you might try one using your front brakes. Ride your bike at medium speed. Have your weight just off the seat. Then stand high on the pedals and shift your weight over your handlebars. Squeeze your front brake and push down on your handlebars. Shift your weight to the back wheel and—hold it!

An endo in freestyling means your rear wheel is off the ground.

The Bunny Hop

Bunny hops are usually the first kind of jump a BMX rider—racer or freestyler—learns. Start by hopping small items: first a small box, then a pile of old newspapers.

Ride at medium speed. Lower your body over the bike as you get near your object. Keep your pedals level and keep your feet on them. When you are about a bike-length away from your object, begin to move up off the saddle. At the same time, pull the front end up as if you were popping a wheelie.

For a split second, it will look as if you are going to hit your object. But, as you seem about to hit it, slide back over your rear wheel, bend your knees, and push forward and down on the handlebars. This movement brings your rear wheel up. Practice the slide-bend-push forward and down until it is a smooth, rolling, coordinated movement. When you get the correct rhythm, you'll sail right over the object. As you practice, you'll fly higher and higher.

The first kind of jump a BMX rider learns is the bunny hop.

The more you practice, the higher you will be able to "fly".

The Pogo

The **pogo** is a bicycle's imitation of a pogo stick—repeated bounces or jumps. (The pogo is a basic freestyling jump, so be sure you've got the right kind of bike.)

Start by standing with one foot on the back pedal to set the rear coaster brake. Put your other foot on the other pedal. Lean back and pull up on the handlebars. (You'll feel like you're ready to do a wheelie.) Your coaster brake should stay on.

Flex or spring your body up and pull the bike with you. Keep the front end high, then stretch out your body and pull the whole bike off the ground. The harder you pull and lift, the higher you'll pogo. Keep repeating the movements and you'll keep pogo-ing!

Once you can do the pogo, you might want to add a 180° (half-turn) turn. As you pull up on your handlebars and straighten your legs, twist the bike a half-turn as it lifts off the ground. Keep turning with your arms and legs stretched out. Land softly by bending into the bike again.

The pogo is a basic freestyle jump.

CONCLUSION

Around the racetrack or through the air, flying a bicycle is great fun. You've chosen a sport that's growing and changing every day. And, with practice, you'll grow and change with it. So—helmets on! Good flying!

Many BMX riders enter competitions, but many more ride and "fly" their bikes just for fun.

GLOSSARY

alloy - a metal that is a mixture of two or more other metals

bar hop - (freestyle) a move in which the rider puts his or her legs through his or her hands and over the handlebars while the bike is moving

berm - the dirt bank on any turn

caliper brakes - hand brakes

coaster brake - pedal brake; a rider activates this brake by pedaling a half-turn in reverse

crash and burn - fall off your bike

endo - in racing, an over-the-handlebars fall; in freestyling, tipping forward on the front wheel

frame stand - (freestyle) balancing on the bike frame while the bike is moving forward

holeshot - (racing)lead position at the bottom of the starting ramp

knobby - a tire with very pronounced tread

moto - a single race

obstacle - any bump, jump, low wall, fence, or other object put on a racetrack to test racers

pogo - (freestyle) continuous bouncing on one or both bike wheels

quarterpipe - a specially-curved ramp

rad riding - tricky or unusual performance

ramp - (freestyle) a slanted wooden or concrete surface; used for gaining height or speed

recovery - pulling out of a bad move

sweeper - a sharp, flat curve that has no banking; also called a *hairpin*

tactics - plans and moves for winning a race

tabletop - (racing) a track obstacle that has a flat top

taking air - (freestyling) a position in which both wheels are off the ground

thrashing - non-competitive neighborhood riding or styling on a BMX bike

wheelstand - (freestyle) a no-hands stand on the front wheel of your bike when it is turned 90° off center (perpendicular to the bike)

whoop-de-doos - a series of bumps in the track

wipeout - lose control of bike; "crash and burn"